Dying Fo
The Martyro
Church

MW01491611

First printing, 2015

ISBN-13: 978-1511995610

Printed in the United States of America

Dedicated to Jesus the Messiah, the God of Abraham, Isaac, and Jacob. To His Glory and Honor.

I want to thank my Mother and Father for editing and helping to publish this work. I want to thank my Grandmother for editing this book multiple times. I also want to thank my sister, Emma for contributing a photograph. Finally, I want to thank my family for all their encouragement, prayers, and support!

May God be glorified with this book.

Soli Deo Gloria

DYING FOR THE TRUTH:

The Martyrdom of the Apostles of the Early Church

Jesse D. Dieterle

Table of Contents

Introduction   7

Chapter 1: James, the Son of Zebedee   10

Chapter 2: Peter, Son of Jonas   14

Chapter 3: John, the Son of Zebedee   20

Chapter 4: Simon the Zealot   25

Chapter 5: Thomas   29

Chapter 6: Matthias   34

Chapter 7: Matthew, the Son of Alphaeus   39

Chapter 8: Bartholomew (Nathanael)   44

Chapter 9: Philip   50

Chapter 10: Andrew   56

Chapter 11: James, the Son of Alphaeus   61

Chapter 12: Thaddeuas (Judas)   66

Chapter 13: James, the Brother of Jesus   73

Chapter 14: Paul, the Apostle   81

Conclusion   103

Introduction

"It is the cause, not the death, that makes the martyr."

Napoleon Bonaparte, Emperor of the French, (1769-1821)

Tetelestai! When Jesus, our Savior, spoke these last words, took his last breath on the Cross and died,   persecution was launched against Christians throughout the world for twenty-one centuries. Persecution of   Christians will always be around until the end of the age, because of our faith in Christ. Jesus declared in Luke 21:17, "All men will hate you because of me."[1] Matthew 24:9 states, "Then shall they deliver you up to be afflicted, and shall kill you: and ye shall be hated of all nations for my name's sake."[2] Luke 21:16, it says, "You will be   betrayed even by parents, brothers, relatives and friends, and they will put some of you to death."[3]

 A Martyr is defined as "a person who willingly suffers death rather than renounce his or her religion."[4] Once in Heaven these courageous Christians will be adorned with the crown of life. Revelation 2:10 says, " Be thou faithful unto death, and I will give thee a crown of life."[5] These early martyrs of our faith are evidence that Jesus is the real and true Messiah. A man would not lose his life for a belief, if he did not regard the ideology as truth or if it was a lie made up by himself and fellow conspirators. Why would Onesiphorus, the Apostle Paul's friend, choose to die a brutal death, being tied to wild horses, dragged, and torn to pieces, if Jesus was a false or fraud Messiah? The Son of God isn't a counterfeit. He is the Savior of the World.

These martyrs inspire us to be like them. The persecution they endured led them into an intimate walk with God their Savior. Some were preaching as they faced death and many were joyful as they faced martyrdom for they knew they would meet their Savior in Heaven. Learning about these martyred saints will give us faith in our own walk with God and strength to face any persecutions in our own life. The martyrdom of the Apostles shows us their strong faith in Jesus, their loving spirits to the end of their days, and their persistence to share the gospel at the cost of their very lives.

Chapter 1
James, the Son of Zebedee
Martyred in 44 A.D.

"Whatever you are, be a good one."

Abraham Lincoln, 16th President of the United States, (1809-1865)

James was a fisherman by trade and the son of Zebedee and Salome. He first met Jesus, when the Messiah called him and his brother, John, to be "Fishers of Men." In Mark 3:17, Jesus calls James and his brother the "Sons of Thunder,"[1] because of their brutal tempers; however, the Lord can change anyone's heart. As a disciple, James learned all he could about this world and the next. James, John, and Peter were Jesus' main and most loved disciples. James was a man of great faith, who shared the Gospel with exceptional zeal. Like Jesus, he preached to the Jews first and then the Gentile. After preaching to Judea and Samaria, tradition says he went to preach in Spain and then travelled back to Judea where James was martyred. This would fulfill a prophecy spoken by the Prophet Agabus in Acts 11:27-28, "And in these days came prophets from Jerusalem unto Antioch. And there stood up one of them named Agabus, and signified by the Spirit that there should be great death throughout all the world: which came to pass in the days of Claudius Caesar."[2] It would be fulfilled in the fourth year of the Roman Emperor,

Claudius, who declared to Herod Agrippa I to persecute this new sect called the Christians. Now, Herod captured two apostles: Peter and James. He put James in prison before Passover. Peter escaped to tell the story to his praying friends. James would be beheaded at the decree of Herod Agrippa I, before Passover. This death sentence was decreed before Passover, because it was against the law to kill a man, during this biblical feast. Tradition says that while the Apostle was being taken to his death, Alexandrinus, the executioner, was touched by James' faith. He asked sorrowfully for the apostle's forgiveness. James proclaimed, " Peace be with thee"[3] and gave him a kiss. The executioner proclaimed that he had become a Christian. Romans 8:28 proclaims that God works "all things for good." He used James' death to bring eternal life to Alexandrinus. Together, James and Alexandrinus were beheaded and went to Heaven to be eternally with their Savior. James was the second martyr of the Christian faith. Stephen was the first. James, the son of Zebedee, was the first apostle to be martyred.

Mark 10:38-39 sheds light on why James was the first apostle to die. Jesus asked James and John, "Can you drink the cup I drink or be baptized with the baptism I am baptized with? 'We can,' they answered."[4] The cup signifies suffering or persecution which these two brothers endured for Jesus. They truly knew what Paul meant in Philippians 1:21, " For to me, to live is Christ and to die is gain."[5] After his martyrdom, James went to Heaven and saw his Savior again. One day he will be given his martyr's crown.

Chapter 2
Peter or Simon,
the Son of Jonas,
Martyred in 67-68 A.D.

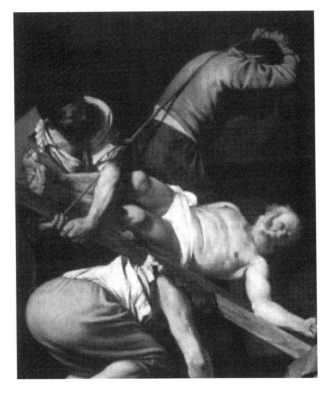

"Jesus is everything."
Mother Teresa, Roman Catholic missionary
to India, (1910-1997)

Peter was born to Jonas in Bethsaida, located in the northern part of Israel known as Galilee. He and his family were fishermen. Andrew and Peter made a fishing partnership with John and James, the sons of Zebedee. Andrew and John brought their older brothers to Christ, after meeting and believing in Jesus.

Jesus renamed Peter, because Simon (his original name) means shifting sand or unstable one. Peter, because of his new belief, was given the name Cephas, which means "Rock" in Aramaic. Jesus wants us to stand firm in our belief in Him. God makes us a new person, when we're born again.

Shortly afterwards, Peter, his brother and friends were commanded by Jesus to leave their jobs. Now this partnership was after new game. They were fishers of men! After Jesus died, Peter became strong and firm in his belief. He was a leader in this group. Peter was part of Jesus' three favorite disciples along with James and John.

During Pentecost, they received the Holy Spirit. At this divine event, three thousand became Christians. Later on, the Jewish priests sentenced the twelve Apostles to be flogged for preaching about Jesus. They were not depressed, but rejoicing over this persecution, because they knew they were worthy enough to be tortured for Christ. God's purpose was underway. Jews and Gentiles were being brought to Christ.

Herod Agrippa I wanted to destroy this new sect by killing the leaders. He captured Peter and put him in prison under heavy guard. Four soldiers guarded Peter. The most dangerous of criminals were only watched by two guards. His Christian companions were praying desperately for him, because of James' recent martyrdom. God heard the prayers of his companions and a divine miracle took place. In the middle of the night, an angel of the Lord appeared and freed Peter from his impending death. The chains that bound him fell off a half awakened Peter. The angel took him out of the dark, dreary prison without waking a single person.

Peter must have been amazed, when enormous, heavy doors just opened miraculously. Once set free, the angel suddenly vanished from sight. Peter went to where his companions were praying for him. Rhoda opened the door and was shocked to see that it was him. Jon Courson emphasizes that "Prayer was made on Peter's behalf, and what a difference it would make! What would have happened had the believers prayed when James was in prison? I wonder. Why didn't the church pray for James? Perhaps they thought, *Why pray? God's will is going to be done anyway.* The Bible says we have not because we ask not (James 4:2)."[1] The prayers for Peter's rescue were powerful and miraculous.

Tradition says Peter went to Greece to spread the words of Jesus to the Corinthians. He later went on to preach in Rome. Many believe that Peter was also the first Bishop of Rome. Just before his death, he wrote the books of the Bible we know today as 1st and 2nd Peter.

Peter was one of the many Christians martyred by Nero. In Rome, in 64 A.D., a fire destroyed ten of Rome's fourteen districts. The people of the city where outraged. Emperor Nero wished for the destruction of a new sect of Jews, who believed in a messiah named Jesus Christ. The emperor used the people's outrage and his will to blame the Christians for the fire. In truth, the Christians were only scapegoats, but in reality, Nero was the one who ignited the fire. Christians were martyred in mass numbers including Peter and Paul, Christ's Apostles.

The night before Peter's martyrdom some companions told him to escape. He made the successful break from the cold, dark, damp Roman prison. Led by the Spirit, Peter took the Great Appian Road and met the last person he would be likely to meet. It was Jesus! Herbert Lockyer retells the tradition of that conversation. "I had a disciple who was imprisoned there, and was to be put to death. He is escaped and is free. I go to die a second time, for him." Peter cried " Lord go not: I will return and die!"[2] Peter went back the next day to be martyred. He was crucified by the evil Emperor Nero. Origen, the great Church leader, observes Peter's death, "When he was brought to the cross he made the request, " Not with my head up: My Master died that way! Crucify me head down-ward. I die for my Lord: but I am not worthy to die like Him."[3] This gives historical evidence to Jesus' prophecy of Peter's death in John 21:18-19, "Truly, truly, I say to you, when you were young, you used to dress yourself and walk wherever you wanted, but when you are old, you will stretch out your hands (this indicates crucifixion), and another will dress you and carry you where you do not want to go (This he said to show by what kind of death he was to glorify God with)."[4] Peter was taken by the Roman soldiers who nailed his hands and feet, just like his Savior. This great man of God was placed upside down on the cross. The old apostle denied not his Savior with his last act of love for Jesus Christ. Peter was martyred in humbleness and love for Jesus. He was killed, but glorified and honored his Lord and Savior. Peter is a true

Christian hero and in his death manifested the love and peace of Christ. Peter will enjoy Heaven with the One he has always loved and served.

Chapter 3
John, the Son of Zebedee, Died in 101 A.D.

"My Dear Jesus, my Savior, is so deeply written in my heart, that I feel confident, that if my heart were to be cut open and chopped to pieces, the name of Jesus would be found written on every piece." Ignatius, a student of John who was martyred by lions, (35-108 A.D.)

John was born to Zebedee and Salome around the 1st century A.D. and like his brother James was a fisherman. John and Andrew heard the message of Christ and had the faith to believe in the Messiah. The first people they brought to Christ were their older brothers. John was very special. He was Jesus' favorite and most loved of all the disciples. He was the only one who stayed with Jesus to the very last moment of his death. John did not fear his life like the rest of his fellow believers. He witnessed the empty tomb and believed with all his heart that Jesus rose from the dead.

John wrote many books of the Bible: John, 1 John, 2 John, 3 John, and Revelation. Through the inspiration of the Holy Spirit, he wrote the book of John, because his fellow Christians kept asking him to write this amazing story of love. Many Jews came to know Christ through the Gospel of John, because the first verse parallels the beginning verse of Genesis.

Many traditions have been told about John. It is recorded that he wore a gold plate tied to his forehead like a Jewish High Priest, which was inscribed with the words " Holiness to the Lord."[1] Another tradition says that someone poisoned his drink, but he didn't die, because he had God's protection. One tradition, called the Latin Gate, happened during the reign of the evil persecutor Domitian, who had the nerve to call himself God. Domitian hated Christians. Domitian captured John and had him put into boiling oil, but John was neither burned nor scared. God placed his hand over his favorite disciple. John remarked that the boiling oil was like a bath and returned him to a youthful feeling. Domitian was so angry that he couldn't kill John and had him exiled to the Island of Patmos in the Aegean Sea. The Romans sent him here, because as Jon Courson declares, it's "where the most perverted people, the most incorrigible prisoners were sent. A rocky, barren island, it was the most hell-like place the Roman Empire knew about."[2] If John was killed in Rome by the bubbling oil, he would have never received the vision of End Times and penned the book of Revelation.

Later, after the death of Domitian, an Emperor named Nerva came to power. During his short reign, he freed John who then went to Ephesus, modern day Turkey. In this city, John spent the rest of his life discipling believers. John discipled three famous apostolic fathers: Polycarp, Papias, and Ignatius. They all made reference to John's loving and humble life. John spent the remainder of his days on Earth spreading the Christian love Jesus taught him.

One tradition states that John died and was buried in a tomb, but resurrected by Jesus, the Messiah. Many say he died around 101 A.D. during the reign of the Roman Emperor Trajan in Ephesus, Asia Minor. Some believe that John never died, but like Enoch and Elijah, was brought to Heaven, because of his strong walk with God.

John felt very lonely. He missed his old friends and looked forward to seeing Jesus in Heaven. John died a peaceful death at the age of 100 with all his disciples around him. Daniel Mclean declares that with his death, "He crowned the apostolic age,"[3] because he was the last of Jesus' twelve Disciples to die.

When John went to Heaven, he experienced everything he saw and wrote about in his vision. John was loved a great deal by Jesus and used his whole life in the service of God. When John gets his crown in Heaven, Jesus will declare to him " Well done good and faithful servant. (Matthew 25:23)" [4]

Chapter 4
Simon, the Zealot
Martyred in 65 A.D.

"How sweet is rest after fatigue!

How sweet will heaven be when our journey is

ended."

George Whitefield, 18th century English

evangelist, (1714-1770)

Simon the Zealot was born in Galilee in northern Israel. Not much is known about Simon except from the Bible and tradition. "Simon" in Hebrew means "hearing". He heard the word of Jesus and believed. Many say he was part of the Zealots, a group of Jews trying to overthrow the Roman occupation, who were cruelly governing their land. The Zealots would use whatever measures possible to kick out these "impostors." He might have been from the city of Cana or the region of Canaan, because he was also called Simon the Canaanite. "Canaanite" in Aramaic means "zealous one."

One tradition says Simon was the groom at the wedding in Cana, where Jesus turned water into wine. God was able to bring two people, Simon and Mathew, with different mindsets together. Jon Courson writes, "If Simon the Zealot and Matthew, who was employed by the Romans, had met in any other circumstance, Simon would have put a knife in Matthew's back. But here Jesus brings them together. Just like us!"[1] In the pamphlet "12

Disciples" by Rose Publishing, the author states a key lesson for us from Simon's life, " One should be willing to sacrifice his or her politics to follow Jesus."[2]

Simon had great zeal for the Lord and witnessed Jesus' amazing miracles and resurrected body. After receiving the Holy Spirit, the Apostles chose lots to decide which person would evangelize each part of the world. Simon's lot was Mesopotamia, Syria, Edessa (Greece), and Arabia. However, the Apostles went beyond their specified region to evangelize to more people. Simon preached the Gospel to countries beyond his lot including: Egypt, Cyrene (Northern Africa), Mauritania, Libya, and England. After Simon landed on the Island of Great Britain and preached there, he joined his fellow friend and Apostle Thaddeus, in Persia.

Simon the Zealot and Thaddeus became a missionary team, working together for the glory and service of saving souls for Jesus. Simon and Thaddeus went into the Parthian Empire beginning at Babylon and going North to Persia. The empire was split into two parts between two brothers, Vardana in Babylon, and Nerseh in Persia.

These two missionaries were martyred in the North (Persia) in the city of Colchis. They were put to death by furious priests, because their followers were straying from their past, pagan religion. These pagan priests took Simon's body and with a jagged, razor, tipped saw they split him in two from head to toe.

Herbert Lockyer says this about Simon, " This apostle, conspicuous for his zeal and burning enthusiasm, who came to learn of the purer, deeper, and stronger zeal of the Master (Jesus) he followed."[3] God worked mightily in Simon the Zealot and changed his attitude from this world to the next. Simon will be casting his crowns at the feet of our Savior.

Chapter 5
Thomas
Martyred in 53 A.D.
or 72 A.D.

"Afflictions are light when compared with what we really deserve. They are light when compared with the sufferings of the Lord Jesus. But perhaps their real lightness is best seen by comparing them with the weight of glory which is awaiting us."
Arthur W. Pink, English evangelist and Bible scholar, (1886-1952)

Thomas was born in the beautiful, hilly, grasslands of Galilee. Some people say he was a fisherman like Peter, Andrew, James, and John. Thomas displayed his love for Jesus when he declared in John 11:16, that he would go to Jerusalem to die with Jesus. This proclamation shows a great amount of courage!

Thomas was not with the disciples, when they saw Jesus resurrected. Jon Courson explains that Thomas wasn't there, because "The other guys (disciples) were hiding in the Upper Room while Thomas was the only one who had the guts to be out on the streets."[1]Thomas was preaching even after Jesus' death even though he could have been killed. Thomas was brave and stood up for Jesus in one of the toughest times.

While Thomas was preaching, his fellow disciples witnessed Jesus in his resurrected form. Thomas couldn't believe what his friends experienced and testified. Thomas then pronounced in John 20:25 that he would believe if he "shall see in his hands the print of the nails, and put my finger into the print of the nails, and thrust my hand into his side. "[2] Thomas was very faithful to Jesus, but didn't have much faith in what could happen through his Lord.

Eighty days later, Jesus appeared to them in his resurrected body. John 20:27 declares, " Then he said to Thomas put your finger here; see my hands. Reach out your hand and put it into my side. Stop doubting and believe."[3] Jesus was answering Thomas' request, so that he would believe that his Messiah rose from the dead. Through this interaction, Jesus teaches us the lesson that God is with us all the time, even when He feels far away.

After Pentecost, the Apostles chose lots that would direct them to where they were to preach the Gospel. Thomas' lot included Parthia, Ethiopia, and India. Thomas was afraid to go to India. Its evil religion made those people cruel. However, the Lord had other plans. Jesus appeared to Thomas and said, "Fear not, Thomas, go thou unto India, and preach the word there, for my grace is with thee."[4] Thomas didn't have enough money for a passage on a ship, so he hired himself as a slave to an Indian merchant, who sold him to the King of India. Thomas humbled himself and followed the Lord whole heartily to save those who would believe in Jesus. Once he got to his destination, he began to preach in India. The pagans told him to stop preaching, but he continued to listen to God's plans.

God was with Thomas as he preached throughout the wealthy, but sinful country of India. Thomas was working powerfully in India, but even when good is happening Satan is always fighting against you. Thomas angered the priests of India, because he was leading their followers to Christ. Tradition says that while Thomas was either praying or preaching in Bombay the immoral priest (or four soldiers) of the city came and drove a spear through him. Thomas was faithful to the end.

Another tradition says that in Calamina, India, with God's help, Thomas was bringing the people away from the sun god to the Son of God. The evil priests were gnashing their teeth and clinching their hands in anger. Then these insidiously, angry priests brought Thomas before their furious and outraged king, who happily sentenced him to death. First, Thomas was tortured with red-hot plates, but did not renounce his faith in the Lord. Then, he was put into a fiery furnace, but amazingly, like Shadrach, Meshach, and Abednego, was not touched or hurt by the scorching flames. This miracle angered the priests so much that they struck him in the side with javelins and there he died in the blazing fire.

In Heaven, Thomas will receive a martyr's crown. Thomas, now in His presence, sees his Lord's body pierced through with holes and now sees the resurrected Messiah without a doubt, but with a believing, loving, and faithful spirit.

Chapter 6
Matthias
Martyred in 70 A.D.

"I will live for God. If no one else does, I
will."
Jonathan Edwards, 18th century
American Evangelist, (1703-1758)

Matthias, most likely, was born in the region around the gorgeous, but hot sea of Galilee. In the book *The Martyr's Mirror,* the author explains Matthias's lineage and tutelage. " According to the opinion of some, Matthias was of the royal house of David; and from his youth was well instructed in the Law of God (Old Testament)."[1] Another thought is that Matthias was one of the 70 disciples. Luke 10:1 states, " The Lord appointed them... and sent them two by two ahead of Him into every city and place where He Himself would go."[2] Clement of Alexandria believed the tradition that says, Matthias, was Zacchaeus (the man who stood on a tree to see Jesus).

After our Lord was crucified for our sins, Judas Iscariot, one of the twelve disciples, was driven to suicide. The eleven Apostles cast lots to choose a replacement for the deceased Judas. Casting lots was a very regular practice during Old Testament times, in order to get an answer from God. For example, the sailors cast lots to see who God was angry with and Jonah's lot was chosen. In New

Testament times, we are to seek God's guidance through the Holy Spirit, not by lots.

There were two choices to fill Judas's place: Matthias and Joseph, who was called Barnabas. Both were with Jesus during his ministry and witnessed His resurrection. The chosen lot was Matthias. Jon Courson believes, " God's choice was neither man. Revelation 21:14 tell us that the names of the apostles are written on the twelve foundations in heaven. My personal conviction is that we won't see Matthias's name on any of those foundations. We'll see Paul's name. I believe Paul was the one who should have filled Judas's office."[3] If the Apostles waited a little longer, God would have chosen Paul to fill the empty position of Judas. Matthias was with the other apostles and received the Holy Spirit with them on the day of Pentecost. Even though Paul was supposed to fill Judas' place, God still worked and used Matthias for His glory and honor.

Matthias first preached to Judea, because Jesus declared that His name be preached to the Jew first and then the Gentile. Jerome, the translator of the Vulgate, the Latin Bible, believed from history that Matthias, after preaching in Judea, went to spread the Salvation message in Ethiopia. It is believed Matthias went farther into the savage wasteland of the Ethiopian Kingdom than any other of his fellow Believers. After his ministry to the Ethiopians, it is recorded by word of mouth, that he either returned to Judea the palatinate of the Romans or went to Cappadocia, modern day Turkey.

At one of these two destinations, there are two stories of Matthias' martyrdom. Matthias went to preach the Gospel to the Cappadocians, the uncivilized, brutish, gentile Greeks of modern day Turkey. The people of Cappadocia were not pleased with this new religion or sect Matthias was sharing in their community. The Cappadocians like many other people groups around the world despised Christianity. To get rid of this new religion in their city, they stoned Matthias and then inhumanly beheaded him.

The other tradition states that when Matthias returned to Judea from Ethiopia, he began to preach to all of Israel including the Samaritans. The Levite priest of the city of Jerusalem did not like Matthias preaching throughout their holy city. The Jews put him to death, because they believed he committed the sin of blaspheming the Torah, the Prophets, and the Writings, but their eyes were veiled. The preaching of Matthias was truth, but the Jews could not see the light of Righteousness. Later that day, Matthias was taken outside Jerusalem and put upon a cross. After, Matthias was taken down from the cross and then stoned. God was with Matthias. After the Apostle's stoning, he was taken to an executioner, who was standing with a long sword that gleamed in the bright sun. The soldiers put Matthias's head on a tree stump and the powerful executioner raised the sword, let the heavy, razor-edged blade fall, and beheaded the spirit-filled Apostle. Matthias' death meant he was passing on to his real home, Heaven, where he would receive a white robe for his martyrdom. Matthias knew that death is the gain of eternal life with Christ Jesus forever and ever.

Chapter 7
Matthew or Levi, the Son of Alphaeus,
Martyred circa 70 A.D.

"Death is only a grim porter to let us into
a stately palace."
Richard Sibbes, Anglican Theologian,
(1577-1635)

Matthew, the son of Alphaeus, was a tax collector for the Roman government, He is possibly the brother of the Apostle James. "The Twelve Disciples" according to Rose Publishing states Matthew's name in Hebrew means "Gift of God."[1] The author David Down believes Matthew lived "At Capernaum and was a.... Levitical priest who had degenerated so far to become a tax collector."[2] Matthew could raise the taxes as high as he wanted, in order to secure the quota that the Romans wanted to receive. Matthew could keep the rest. This future Apostle was most likely a very wealthy man like Zacchaeus. The Jewish people hated the tax collectors of their own blood. They betrayed them by helping their conquerers, the Romans, and cheated them by raising their taxes higher than they were supposed to be. These tax collectors were possessed by money and greed. In the article, Bible Characters: Matthew A Disciple it says, "Tax collectors were creative in finding ways to tax the people. Luke 3:13 states, 'They overcharged [and] brought false charges of smuggling in the hope of extorting hush-money.'

Other ways of making money included taxes on axles, wheels, animals, roads, highways and admission to markets. Some even charged pedestrians taxes."[3]

One day Jesus came to the city of Capernaum, where Matthew lived and worked. This day would change his life forever. Jesus spoke to him, "Follow Me" and Matthew did for the rest of his life. Matthew had so much joy that he made a great feast for Jesus and the disciples.

After the death of Jesus the Messiah, Matthew cast lots like his fellow Apostles in Christ, to split up the world, in order to spread the Gospel as their Savior commanded. Matthew's lot fell upon the evil, inhumane country of Ethiopia. Before going to this country in northern Africa, he preached in Judea for eight years. Jesus says to Paul and the rest of the Apostles in Romans 2:10 "First for the Jew, then for the Gentile."[4] After preaching to the Jews some say Matthew went to preach in Palmyra, modern day Syria, then to the Medes of modern day Iran, and

Parthia of modern day Iran. Another tradition says that he went with Andrew to the the Black sea in Asia Minor,Turkey, where they preached to cannibals. Most likely he went to preach in Ethiopia and Arabia (Yemen, Oman, Sadia Arabia, Kuwait, and Jordan) and there he wrote one of the four Gospels.

The Gospel of Matthew teaches that God came to earth in the flesh and He died for our sins. Matthew's first chapter shows us how Jesus came directly through the Jewish line of Abraham, Jacob, Judah, David and even Zerubbabel. In the article Bible Characters: Matthew A Disciple it says,"Matthew was probably fluent in Greek and Aramaic. Greek was the official language, while Aramaic was the local dialect. Matthew was literate and an educated writer and scribe. It is also believed that he knew a form of shorthand called tachygraphy. This may be the reason he was able to write the detailed accounts of Christ's oral sermons, including the long Sermon on the Mount."[5]

During the time of Matthew's missionary work in Nad Davar, Ethiopia, King Aeglippus died. His successor, Hytacus, a pagan, hated Christians and persecuted Matthew who kept preaching as Jesus commanded. King Hytacus was so sadistic and so cruel that he nailed Matthew's body to the sandy, searing, hot ground and then violently beheaded him. Matthew's blood covered the ground just as his Savior's blood covered his sin decades before.

Matthew, even though he knew he was to be martyred, loved on the Ethiopians just as Jesus loved him when he was a cheating tax collector. Love is the most powerful tool a Christian has.

Matthew will be in Heaven where Jesus will see this tax collector and the amazing work he has done to further Christ's kingdom. Matthew will receive his rewards for following the Lord. The most important thing is that he is living eternally in the majesty and glory of God.

Chapter 8
Bartholomew also known as Nathanael
Martyred circa 70 A.D.

"Expect great things from God. Attempt great
things for God."
William Carey, Baptist missionary to India,
(1761-1834)

Bartholomew was born in Cana in Galilee. The author of *Martyrs Mirror* believes Bartholomew was " Of royal descent, and the nephew of the king of Syria."[1] The Apostle Phillip came to his friend Bartholomew to bring him to Christ, but Bartholomew wouldn't believe. Jon Courson says Nathanael was, "A student of Scripture, who knew the promise of Micah 5:2, which stated that the Messiah would come not from Nazareth, but from Bethlehem."[2] Bartholomew didn't know Jesus was born in Bethlehem and then later moved to Nazareth. Bartholomew went with his friend Phillip to meet Jesus, even though he didn't believe Christ was the Messiah. When Nathanael met the Lord, John 1:48, ""How do you know me?" Nathanael asked. Jesus answered, "I saw you while you were still under the fig tree before Philip called you."[3] In Jesus' day, students traditionally studied under fig trees. The fig tree is the national symbol of Israel. Jon Courson believes that under the fig tree Nathanael was very likely studying Genesis 28— the story of Jacob in the wilderness. "Although it has been said that the softest pillow is a good conscience, fearing for his life because of his treachery and deceit, Jacob used a rock. As he slept, he saw a ladder extending from the heavens to the earth, with angels ascending and descending upon it. 'Truly God is in this place and I knew it not,' Jacob declared. That's why, in the midst of his study of Genesis 28, Jesus approached Nathanael, calling him an Israelite in whom there is no guile, or no 'Jacob.'"[4] This future Apostle was reading this specific passage in the Bible, which the Lord inspired thousands of years before.

In John 1:49, Bartholomew immediately understands that Jesus is the Messiah and answered saying, "Rabbi, thou art the Son of God; thou art the King of Israel."[5] Bartholomew, a student of the Word, knew that Jesus was fulfilling the Old Testament scripture by His actions and deeds.

In Hebrew, Nathanael means "God has given" and God gave Bartholomew salvation. Bartholomew teaches us a lesson through his life. According to the " Twelve Disciples" by Rose Publishing, "

Believers are called to test all things with the Scripture and remain true to its principles."[6]

After Jesus' crucifixion and Pentecost, the Apostles split the world up according to God's will by using lots. The will of God for Bartholomew was to preach to Lycaonia (modern day Turkey), Syria, Northern Asia, India, and Great Armenia. Initially, he went to Turkey and Syria and preached to Gentiles.

One tradition shares that after Nathanael went to Northern Asia, he preached in India where he brought the Gospel of Matthew with him. One hundred and fifty years later, Christians found this Gospel, which Bartholomew had used to teach the Indians. Most likely, Bartholomew and Thomas worked together in India. Many of the Apostles, such as Paul and Barnabas, teamed up to evangelize the world.

After preaching in Asia, Bartholomew went to Armenia (next to modern day Turkey) where he preached in its capital, Albanopolis. Some say he converted King Polymius (King of Armenia) and King Astyages' (King of Babylon) brother, wife, and children. King Astyages became furious with Nathanael, when twelve cities fell away from idol worship. Jesus was working mighty miracles bringing many to Christ. *Martyr's Mirror* says the Armenians, " Through the idol Ashtaroth... the devil was worshiped."[7] Their priests protested to King Astyages that Bartholomew was destroying their religion. Bartholomew was brought before the king to be tried. *Martyr's Mirror* says, "The king... (said) that he (Nathanael) had perverted his brother...Bartholomew had replied... saying that he had not perverted, but converted his brother."[8] The king told Bartholomew to stop preaching about his God, but Bartholomew declared, "that he would rather seal his testimony with blood, than suffer the least shipwreck of his faith."[9] The king, in his rage, sentenced the death of this Apostle.

First, Nathanael was persecuted by the pagans, in Armenia, who beat him with rods. After this savage beating, he was crucified head down like his fellow Apostle Peter. God was with Nathanael and helped him through this persecution. Then the weakened, half dead Nathanael was taken off the cross and flayed by his persecutors. This torture is when someone's skin is peeled off or when one is beaten so severely that skin is removed from their body. Bartholomew loved God so much that he endured this for Christ. After this horrific, gory, and cruel torture was completed, the unrecognizable apostle was taken to an open prairie, where he took what was to be his final breath as a large, wide, gunmetal ax fell on Bartholomew's lacerated neck.

Nathanael endured this martyrdom, because he loves Jesus, the King of the Universe, who suffered so much, so we may live with him in Heaven in His glory forever. Bartholomew's name will be written with the rest of the twelve Disciples on the foundations of Heaven. Nathanael will spend the rest of eternity with the One who he served even unto death, the One who loves him, the One who knows him - Jesus, the Son of God.

Chapter 9
Philip
Martyred in 54 A.D.

"The blood of the martyrs is the seed of the church"

Tertullian, An early Christian apologist from Carthage, (160-225 A.D.)

Phillip was born in the beautiful, lush village of Bethsaida (John 1:44) by the Sea of Galilee. He was the third disciple Jesus had chosen. Phillip knew scripture and saw Jesus in the prophecies of the Old Testament. In the "The Twelve Disciples" by Rose Publishing, there is a quote that gives us perspective and an important lesson we could learn from Phillip's life. It says, " All the knowledge in the world does not compare to the truth found in Jesus."[1] The way Phillip lived his life by studying God's Word has shown us that knowledge doesn't compare to wisdom in Christ. Phillip was one of the Apostles who experienced Pentecost, when he and the other believers received the gift of the Holy Spirit. This event allowed these believers in Christ, who only spoke one language, to speak in foreign languages and bring three thousand to the Savior of the world.

After Pentecost, the Twelve Apostles cast lots to determine God's will for each man. Phillip was sent to spread the Gospel of Jesus Christ to Phrygia (Central Turkey), Syria, Northern Asia, Asia Minor

(Turkey), and Scythia (Central Asia, Eastern Europe, and Northern Caucasus). Martyr's Mirror says, "He (Phillip) laid the foundations of faith (Churches and Christ) in many of these cities."[2]

When the Apostles travelled throughout the world, they would usually go alone and preach wherever the Lord sent them. However there were times, when they worked together, like the missionary team of Paul and Barnabas. On one evangelism trip, Philip travelled with his sister Mariamne and the Apostle Bartholomew, who Philip brought to Christ. They preached throughout the countryside of Asia Minor and then witnessed for the Lord in Phrygia. In Phrygia, this team went to the idolatrous city of Hierapolis, where the Phrygians worshiped a humungous serpent. The Phrygians were praising Satan, but Jesus brought these Apostles into this city to turn these people from the king of sin to the King of Life. In the city, one of those who came to Christ was Nicanora, the wife of the proconsul, who was a Roman governor. The proconsul was enraged with Phillip, Mariamne, and Bartholomew.

Like Paul, this missionary team was turning the world upside down for the Lord. These three evangelists were saving the Phrygians from everlasting separation from their Creator. Phillip scolded the Phrygians in love, because he didn't want them to go to Hell for eternity and many came to believe in Christ. This is a lesson for us. To believe in Christ, we must recognize we are sinners, who would be separated from God for eternity, but for the grace of the Lord.

The officials of the city poured out their wrath on Phillip. He was flagellated. This is when a person's body is lashed to pieces with a flagellum, or whip, which has glass, metal, and bone attached to the end of its leather strands. Phillip endured this pain for Christ, because Jesus, the Son of God, suffered the same torture for him. After Phillip's beating, he was sentenced first to prison and then to death. In Roman times, a prisoner would be thrown down a small hole in the floor where he would fall into a small, cramped room underground. There was no light and it stunk from all kinds of things, including animal dung.

Phillip was eventually taken out of the tiny prison and while still blinded by the sun, he was tied to a pillar and stoned to death. *All the Apostles by* Herbert Lockyer says, " As Phillip was being executed the Earth suddenly quaked and when it seemed as if the people were in danger of being swallowed up alive, they bewailed the evident act of divine vengeance upon their idolatry and repented and immediately the Earth closed ."[3]

Another tradition says that Bartholomew and Phillip where crucified upside-down. Phillip began preaching to the crowd from the cross even in the moment of death and pain. Phillip's powerful testimony persuaded the crowd from hate to compassion for the two apostles. The crowd then took Bartholomew off the cross. Phillip stubbornly insisted to die on the cross for his Lord and Savior. This was the will of God for him to be martyred. The final legend is that Phillip was beheaded at the mercy of the Romans.

Phillip, as a believer in Jesus the Messiah, fulfilled the commands of the Lord. In Acts 1:8, Jesus declares, "You will be my witnesses in Jerusalem, and in all Judea and Samaria, and to the ends of the earth."[4] Matthew 28:19 instructs us, "Therefore go and make disciples of all nations."[5] Phillip will live forever and receive glory in Heaven because of his martyred life. Phillip has been bold in his faith and with his martyrdom he has followed the inspired words of Matthew 10:28, "And do not be afraid of those who kill the body but cannot kill the soul."[6]

Chapter 10
Andrew
Martyred circa 70 A.D.

"A flower, if you bruise it under your feet, rewards you by giving you its perfume."

Richard Wurmbrand, Imprisoned for fourteen years in Romania for his faith, (1909-2001)

Andrew was the son of Jonas, a fisherman, and the older brother of Peter. He was born in the luscious, green country of Galilee in Bethsaida. He and his brother would work as fisherman on the turquoise, blue Sea of Galilee. During this time, he became a disciple of John the Baptist and learned of the Messiah to come. The bible tells us of the day that Andrew met Jesus. (John 1:40) "One of the two who heard John speak and followed Him, was Andrew, Simon Peter's brother."[1] After meeting his Messiah, the first person Andrew told about Jesus was his own brother, Peter. John 1:41 says " He found first his own brother Simon and said to him, 'We have found the Messiah.'"[2] In this wonderful act, we see Andrew's love for God and men. He brought his own brother to Christ. Jesus then calls both of Jonas' boys to become "fishers of men."

As Andrew and the other disciples learned of Jesus' future and saw His miracles, they believed in him more and more. Andrew, according to John 6:8-9, was the one who brought the boy with five loaves and two fish that fed the 5,000, who were with

Christ. Andrew was on fire for the Lord bringing myriads of people to have a true faith in Jesus, the Savior of the world. Andrew was faithful to the Lord, but when Jesus was taken to the cross he fled, just like all of the other disciples.

Jesus died and rose again and Andrew was privileged to see his risen Lord. Jesus forgave the Apostles for fleeing and commissioned them to spread the Gospel of Salvation to every nation, people and man, so that everyone would hear of Christ's redemption. On that day of commissioning, Andrew fulfilled God's Word by obediently carrying out Acts 1:8 "you will be my witnesses in Jerusalem and in all Judea and Samaria, and to the end of the earth."[3] He and his fellow brothers in Jesus received the gift of the Holy Spirit and had the power of God. First, Andrew preached with the other disciples on Pentecost and brought 3,000 followers to Christ. Andrew was then led to the countries of Russia and Scotland. After preaching in these countries, he went to Pontus (Anatolia), Galatia (Central Anatolia), Bithynia(Northern

Anatolia), Scythia (Ukraine, Central Asia, Eastern Europe, and Northern Caucasus, Byzantium (Turkey), Thracia (Greece), Macedonia, Thessaly (Greece), and Achaea (Greece). As he preached, the Lord allowed those who heard to see many miracles.

One day the Lord allowed Andrew to understand that he had run the race for Christ and was nearing the finish line. Aegaeas, the Governor of Edessa, proclaimed that Andrew was to be crucified, because he was bringing the people to Jesus and he hated this new religion. The Governor first told Andrew to stop preaching and warned that he would kill him. Andrew responded, "Had I fear of the cross, I should not have preached the majesty and gloriousness of the cross of Jesus."[4] This decree was fulfilled in the city of Patras in Achaea (Greece). Andrew was tied and hung on the cross with thick rope. Andrew was being crucified as his Savior had been decades before. Andrew's cross was different. It was in the shape of an "X" which stretched both his arms and legs. When seeing the cross, Andrew exclaimed, " O beloved cross! I have greatly longed to for thee. I rejoice to see thee erected here. I come to see thee with a peaceful conscience and with cheerfulness, desiring that I, who am a disciple of him who hung on the cross, may also be crucified."[5] Once near the cross the Apostle declared, " The nearer I come to the cross, the nearer I come to God; and the farther I am from the cross, the farther I remain from God."[6] On that cross, Andrew did not stop fulfilling Jesus' Great Commission. On the cross for three days, he gave hope to the Believers in Christ and also brought more to believe in Jesus, the Savior of the world. He told the Christians "I thank my Lord Jesus Christ...(who) used me for a time as an ambassador....Remain steadfast in the word and doctrine which you have received, instructing one another, that you may dwell with God in eternity and receive the fruit of His promises."[7]

Many tried to get Andrew released and taken down from the cross, but Andrew begged God that he might not "dwell again among men, but receive me (him)."[8]

Andrew's dying words where " O My Lord my God! Whom I have known, whom I have loved, to whom I cling, whom I desire to see, and in whom I am what I am."[9] Then the Apostle of Jesus Christ took his final breath and was ushered into his Messiah's presence. Andrew had fulfilled his work on Earth. Jesus had a wonderful plan for Andrew. He brought many to Christ. Andrew's work is finished and he is taking in the fruits of his labor and enjoying it with friends, followers, and most of all, Jesus.

Chapter 11
James, the Son of Alphaeus
Date Unknown for Martyrdom

"He is no fool who gives up what he cannot keep

to gain that which he cannot lose"

Jim Elliot, missionary martyr to Ecuador, (1927-1956)

James was most likely born in the northern region of Galilee to his father, Alphaeus. James is not the same person as James, the Son of Zebedee, and James, the Brother of Jesus. Some scholars believe Mathew, the tax collector, was James' brother, because Mark 2:14 tells us that Mathew's father was Alphaeus too. The scripture says, "Levi son of Alphaeus sitting at the tax collector's booth."[1] Four times in scripture we see James as one of the twelve disciples Jesus Christ chose as His main followers. Mathew 10:5-8 declares, "These twelve Jesus sent out with the following instructions: 'Do not go among the Gentiles or enter any town of the Samaritans. Go rather to the lost sheep of Israel.' As you go, proclaim this message: 'The kingdom of heaven has come near.' Heal the sick, raise the dead, cleanse those who have leprosy, drive out demons. Freely you have received; freely give.'"[2] In this scripture, James and the other disciples are sent out to their lost family, the Jews, preaching the good news of Christ and doing the miracles of the Lord in His power. In their obedience, the twelve disciples are preparing themselves for the Great

Commission, when they will be sent out by Jesus to share the Gospel with all people.

James is written of in scripture again, when he participated in the Last Supper. He was one of 11 disciples, who believed he was going to betray Christ. Matthew 26:20-21 says, "Jesus said, 'Truly I tell you, one of you will betray me.'They were very sad and began to say to him one after the other, "Surely you don't mean me, Lord?"'[3] Later that day, Judas betrayed Jesus and all of the disciples fled the scene, during Messiah's capture. Three days later the disciples were astonished by the stories Mary Magdalene and the other Mary told of seeing Jesus risen from the dead. Jesus visited the disciples to tell these men His will for them, including the Great Commission. James now knew, truly, that Jesus Christ is the Son of God, the Savior, who took away the world's sin. Those who believe in the Messiah will live eternally. Christ rose into heaven 40 days after His crucifixion. Five hundred of His followers, including James, witnessed His ascension into Heaven.

On Pentecost, 50 days after Passover and the death of Jesus, the 12 apostles brought 3,000 people from many different countries, who spoke in many different languages to Christ. As we see in the Book of Acts, the Apostles went their different ways to spread the Gospel of Jesus to the whole world. James is thought to have preached to Judea and Samaria first, since this is what Jesus proclaimed to his followers in Acts 1:8. After preaching in the region of present-day Israel, tradition states James preached in Spain, England and Ireland. James is said to have performed many amazing miracles in all of these countries and he spread the Truth to many. As James finished his work in a specific location based upon God's will, he would leave disciples to keep the message alive in the hearts of those who believed.

Many stories are told of James' martyrdom. One speaks of when James went to Egypt to preach the Gospel. The tradition records that the message of Christ was disturbing to the people of Ostrakine.

They did not want to believe the Truth and the people acted out against this apostle. James was crucified for his faith and nailed to cross for the message he proclaimed throughout the world. An interesting side note is that Matthew, his brother, also preached in Egypt.

James died for Christ, because of the wonderful message of the Cross. As it relates to James' story, Rose Publishing states, " All followers of Jesus can still accomplish the work of God without being in the limelight."[4] When you evangelize, you won't always receive glory and praise on earth. However, in Heaven, James and many others will receive glory beyond imagination, because God was watching their work and their heart. James loved God so much. As the Bible states, he received salvation freely and he freely gave with his own life so all may hear of the wonderful gift of salvation in Jesus, the Son of God and the Savior of the world.

Chapter 12
Thaddeus, also known as Judas
Martyred in 71 A.D.

"I have but one passion—it is He, it is He alone.
The world is the field and the field is the world; and
henceforth that country shall be my home where I
can be most used in winning souls for Christ."
Count Zinzendorf, German noble who lead the Moravians,
(1700-1760)

Thaddeus was born in Banias, near the Sea of Galilee. This city would later become Caesarea Philippi. Most scholars believe his real name was Judas, which means "praise." When he was chosen to become a disciple, Thaddeus praised God. He was most likely named Judas, because of the famous Jewish warrior Judah Maccabee. Judah Maccabee captured the 2nd Temple from the Greeks under Antiochus IV Epiphanies in 165 B.C. This story would become modern-day Hanukkah and the Jews were proud of recapturing their Holy Temple. The Jews honored this hero by naming many of their sons "Judas." Thaddeus, most believe, was his nickname which means "beloved" or "dear to the heart" in Aramaic. Thaddeus is also written as Lebbaeus and has the same meaning. Jerome, the Bible translator from the 4th Century A.D., called Thaddeus, "Trinomius" or the " man with three names." Therefore, Jesus gave "Judas" two nicknames to distinguish him from the hated Judas Iscariot. We see how Jesus loved Thaddeus enough to protect him from man's hate. We see in Thaddeus' names that he was beloved to Christ

and would always praise Him. This is what all
believers want in their walk with Jesus Christ.

Thaddeus, as tradition is told, was a farmer by the
Sea of Galilee, before he was a disciple of Christ.
Another legend says that Thaddeus was a Zealot, a
Jewish group, who fought to throw the Romans out
of Israel, during the time of Jesus. A Latin
manuscript of the Bible mentions his name as
Judas, the Zealot. Jesus really made a very distinct
band of disciples: fishermen, a farmer, tax collector,
Zealots, and many others of different ways of life.

Many believe Judas was a very smart man
speaking Aramaic and Greek. One day Thaddeus'
life was changed forever. He was chosen to be a
disciple for Christ: to learn, experience, and spread
the Gospel of God. Judas was with the other 11
when Jesus sent all of them out to preach to their
Jewish brothers and sisters (Matthew 10:5-8). In
John 14:22-24, we see Judas as a very curious
man asking Jesus why He has not revealed Himself
to the world; "Then Judas (not Judas Iscariot, but

Thaddeus) said, "But, Lord, why do you intend to show yourself to us and not to the world?"Jesus replied, "Anyone who loves me will obey my teaching. My Father will love them, and we will come to them and make our home with them. Anyone who does not love me will not obey my teaching. These words you hear are not my own; they belong to the Father who sent me."[1] In these verses we see Jesus has come to all, but they must believe on their own and truly believe in their heart of Christ's teachings and His death. Rose Publishing says about Thaddeus and his question " Jesus will reveal his truths to believers who follow him."[2]

Judas is mentioned as being present at the Last Supper of Jesus and partaking in Communion. After witnessing this, Thaddeus and the other disciples followed Jesus to the Garden of Gethsemane, where the Lord prayed. Then Jesus was taken away by the Temple soldiers and sadly Thaddeus fled the scene like his fellow disciples.

After the Death of their Messiah, the disciples waited three days in hiding and then they saw their risen Lord. Jesus spent 40 days teaching them and telling the disciples of their mission, before He rose into Heaven to sit down at the right side of the throne of God.

Thaddeus was one of the 500 who witnessed the angels taking Jesus into His eternal palace. After this, he and the disciples brought 3,000 people to Christ on Pentecost. Then the 12 Disciples split up to spread the Gospel to all the World.

Thereafter,Thaddeus began to preach in Judea and Samaria (Acts 1:8). Judas then went to Idumea (Edom or modern-day-Israel and Syria), Syria, Mesopotamia (mostly modern-day Iraq and Iran), Libya, Arabia, Edessa (modern-day Turkey), and Phoenicia.

There are many stories that tell of how Thaddeus was martyred, but I have chosen three of the most believable. First, Simon the Zealot, who is believed to be Judas' brother, and Thaddeus went to Persia. In the city of Colchis, he and his brother angered the pagan priest. The two disciples of Christ were imprisoned for their faith and then both were killed. Thaddeus was taken to a spot, where an executioner stood, and like his brother Simon, his whole body was sawn in half.

Another story states that the King Adgar V of Edessa was stricken with a disease and wrote a letter to Jesus, before His crucifixion, asking Him to come and heal him. Thaddeus went to the city to heal the king, because Jesus had already ascended to Heaven. He was possibly with his brother Simon the Zealot. Judas healed the King through God's power. Soon after, King Adgar and his whole country became the first true Christian nation. King Adgar ruled from 15 B.C.- 50 A.D. and when he died his kingdom was divided between his son and nephew.

King Adgar's nephew had believed in Christ, but rejected the truth, because he feared others and their thoughts of him. No matter how hard your life gets- you must always trust in Jesus Christ. The King's nephew decreed that Thaddeus was to be killed by the pagan priests, because he was preaching the Gospel. It is possible that when Thaddeus died in Edessa, Simon was sawed to death along with his brother. Thaddeus was martyred, when godless priests beat the apostle to death in the street with stones and wooden and iron clubs.

The last story says that Thaddeus went to Phoenicia or the Roman Provence of Syria, without Simon. His preaching angered the people in the city of Beirut. He was taken to the officials and sentenced to death. The apostle of Christ was taken to a wooden stump and his head was severed by an ax.

Regardless of how Thaddeus died, we know that he had a strong will to preach the truth, even if it cost him his life. God blessed his actions on earth by giving him his eternal rewards in Heaven. Now in Heaven, Thaddeus is with Jesus, the one who he preached about, the one who he died for, and most significantly, the One who died for him.

Chapter 13
James, the Brother of Jesus
Martyred in 63 A.D.

"God sweetens outward pain with inward peace."
Thomas Watson, 17th century English Puritan preacher (1620-1686)

James, not to be confused with James, the son of Zebedee or James, the son of Alphaeus, was born to Joseph and Mary in the city of Nazareth around the lush, green region of the Galilee. He was the younger half brother of Jesus. James' childhood must have been amazing as he lived, played, and was loved by his older brother, Jesus. This is a great picture of our lives with Jesus, because He is our older brother protecting and loving us all the time. James had many brothers and sisters. Mark 6:3 states, "Isn't this the carpenter? Isn't this Mary's son and the brother of James, Joseph, Judas, and Simon? Aren't his sisters here with us?"[1]

Many people believe James was not the younger brother of Jesus, but the older brother. There is a belief that Joseph was married to another women before Mary and this woman would have given birth to James. This belief perpetuates the teaching that Mary remained a virgin her entire life. This is not possible. Joseph, a descendant of David, would have taken great pride in his bloodline. He would obviously have had many offspring. Once married to Mary, he would have taken God's Word very seriously when He says, " Be fruitful and multiply."[2] The implications of God's will means Mary would have not been a virgin her entire life. During the 1st Century A.D., most Jews devoutly followed the words and laws of God to the exact jot and tittle.

James would have most likely followed after his father, Joseph, and Jesus by becoming a carpenter. This is what Jon Courson says of Jesus and James, "Can you imagine growing up with a Brother who never did anything wrong, who never called you a name, never teased you, or never made fun of you? Jesus was the nicest brother who ever lived."[3] Between Jesus and James there must of been many fond memories of the two brothers doing everything together. James must have always been following behind his older brother, but soon he would be following Jesus for a totally different reason.

James became a believer afterJesus had died and was resurrected. Many scholars believe Jesus made a special appearance to James. During this experience, Jesus would have explained who He was and that His purpose on earth was to die for the sins of mankind. What an experience to find out your older brother was the Messiah. James believed in Christ and followed His commands. James was with the other followers of Christ when Jesus was taken into Heaven to be with his Father. After this miraculous experience, James, his mother, his brothers, and the apostles prayed together. After praying for many days, these followers drew lots and Matthias was chosen to take Judas Iscariot's place. On Pentecost, James and the apostles spoke to 3,000 people in their native language and these 3,000 people became Believers that day.

Many people have called him "James the Camel-Kneed." James prayed so often that his knee's became as callous as a camel's knee. James is a great representation of Corrie Ten Boom's (1892-1983) quote, "A man is powerful on his knees."[4] In James, we see a very strict and obedient person always wanting to serve God. He was a Nazarite like Paul. Numbers 6:4-6 says, "As long as they remain under their Nazarite vow, they must not eat anything that comes from the grapevine, not even the seeds or skins. During the entire period of their Nazarite vow, no razor may be used on their head. They must be holy until the period of their dedication to the Lord is over; they must let their hair grow long. Throughout the period of their dedication to the Lord, the Nazarite must not go near a dead body." The Nazarite followed their vows in strict obedience to the Lord, the God of all.

James became the leader of the Church of Jerusalem and would be in charge of this church, until his death. While in this position, he would experience severe persecution from his people, the Jews, and he would witness many of his friends being killed, including Stephen and James, the brother of Zebedee. He stayed strong and kept bringing people to Christ even through these difficult times. James was a part of the Jerusalem council as recorded in Acts 15, where the issues concerning Jewish Law and its heavy yoke were resolved. In the end, James created four things to abstain from: idols, sexual immorality, strangled things, and blood. These four rules prevent us from falling into sin, and keep us from continual sin just as the Ten Commandments do. James' job in Jerusalem was to stop disagreements within the church. This is why he was called "James the Just." He fed the church with the Word of God and brought many people to believe in Christ.

Another interesting fact is that he wrote a letter to his fellow Messianic brothers in Christ, who were dispersed throughout the world, encouraging them to be holy. This letter is in the modern-day Bible and is called the Epistle of James. Biblical historians believe the Book of James was written in 46 A.D., which would make this letter the oldest book of the New Testament. This letter contains wisdom for everyone from the Lord. Many teachings from James help believers in their every day life. Herbert Lockyer states, "James' noble epistle, which ever remains a living monument to the faith, character, and wisdom of the brother of our Lord."[5]

After many years of preaching on this earth, God planned for James to finally be taken home to be in peace forever. James was preaching the Gospel of Christ, when he was taken away by the very haughty Pharisees and Sadducees. The High Priest Ananias and his soldiers placed James on the pinnacle of the Temple. Then Ananias stood before a crowd of people and spoke to James asking him to renounce Christ. This event was happening during Passover. Hundreds of thousands of people were waiting at the Temple to sacrifice their offerings for their sins. These people did not know their lambs were not needed. The one and only lamb, Jesus, had already been sacrificed. James, in boldness, spoke to these people about Jesus and how he died for their sins and that now there is no need for sacrifices because their sins had been paid for on the cross. Amazingly, people started to believe in Jesus and praised God. Even in the face of persecution, the Lord uses it for His good.

While James was preaching, Ananias told his soldiers to push the apostle off the pinnacle of the Temple, which was over a 100 feet high. On this same pinnacle, over 30 years before, Satan told Jesus to throw himself down, but He defeated Satan with the Word of God. Now James defeated Satan by speaking the Word of God instead of falling into the deceitful plan of saving his own life. God had appointed James to die, so he may glorify God with this special honor. Even though James fell from such a high height, he did not die. Only his legs were broken. Those callous knees of prayer saved him. In excruciating pain, he kneeled on his broken knees and started to pray.

The sinful, prideful Sadducees and Pharisees began to stone him, but he forgave them and proclaimed that they do not know what they are doing. Miraculously, he did not die and kept praying for those around him. Then someone from the crowd pulled out a long, strong, wooden fullers club and hit him on the side of the head. Instantly, James was ushered into the kingdom of God.

James never doubted God and always used the situation to further the kingdom of God. He's in Heaven enjoying the memories he had with Jesus and also praising His wonderful, powerful name. His love never ends for Christ and he will receive crowns upon crowns for his service to the King of Kings. He died brutally, but for a cause that is for eternity and the future will be longer than the present. James is enjoying the fruits of his ministry, which are still propagating today. In Heaven, James was escorted into the joy of the Lord and is in Jehovah's presence….the One whom he loves with all his heart, soul, and strength.

Chapter 14
Paul, the Apostle
Martyred in 67-68 A.D.

"The highest honor that God can confer upon his children is the blood-red crown of martyrdom. The jewels of a Christian are his afflictions. The regalia of the kings that God has made, are their troubles, their sorrows, and their griefs. Griefs exalt us, and troubles lift us."
Charles Spurgeon, 19th century English preacher
(1834-1892)

Paul was born to very strict Jewish parents in the city of Tarsus, located in Asia Minor (Turkey). Many call him Paul, but that was his Latin name. His Hebrew name was Saul. Saul had to have two names, because his father was a Pharisee and a Roman citizen, which was passed onto Saul by birth and for Roman records he needed a Latin name. Since his father was a strict Pharisee, he was also given a Judaic name. Paul was most likely named after his famous ancestor, King Saul, since his Jewish family was from the tribe of Benjamin. Many historians also believe Paul only used his Latin name, when speaking to the Gentiles, but it seems as if he favored this name, because he uses it in all his Epistles. When he became a Christian, he started using Paul instead of Saul, because he wanted to be known as the new believer in Christ, not Saul who persecuted the followers of Christ.

In Tarsus, besides learning all the Jewish laws and traditions. he learned a trade as a tent maker, which would later fund his mission trips. After a certain amount of time, his Pharisaic parents sent him to Jerusalem to study under the highly famed Rabbi Gamaliel. This is why, in the New Testament, Paul is able to quote so many Biblical references of the Old Testament. In Acts 22:3, we understand more of Paul's time in Jerusalem. He says, "I am a Jew, born in Tarsus of Cilicia, but brought up in this city. Under Gamaliel I was thoroughly trained in the law of our fathers and was just as zealous for God as any of you are today."[1] During this period in Saul's life, he would become like many of the Pharisees of the New Testament. In many ways, the Pharisees, including Paul, were similar to the Orthodox Jews of today. They are all very strict and pious.

Acts 8:1 states " And Saul was there (consenting) …."[2] This means that Saul was a part of the Sanhedrin, during the time of the Early Church, when they were voting to kill Stephen. Jon Courson comments about this scripture, "This Saul, of course, would later be known as the apostle Paul. The word "consenting" actually means "voting," implying that Saul was a voting member of the

Sanhedrin, the Jewish Supreme Court. This interests me, because marriage was one of the requirements for a position on the Sanhedrin—and yet Paul wrote to the church at Corinth that it was good for the unmarried and the widows to remain in a single state even as he was (1 Corinthians 7:8). If Paul was married in Acts and single in 1 Corinthians, what happened to his wife? Some suggest she died, that he was a widower who chose to remain single in order to give himself more fully to ministry. Much more probable, however, based upon the writings of early church history, is that Paul's wife left him, when he was converted. Either way, it's interesting that Paul doesn't tell the story. Truly, he practiced what he preached when he wrote, "Forgetting those things which are behind, and reaching forth unto those things which are before, I press toward the mark for the prize of the high calling of God in Christ Jesus" (Philippians 3:13, 14)."[3]

While Paul was in the Sanhedrin, an event happened which would revolutionize his life. During the early days of the Church, the Apostles chose seven men who would help feed the church so the Apostles could concentrate solely on spreading the Gospel. One of these men was Stephen, who had a faithful heart for the Lord. God allowed blessings to reign down upon Stephen, which allowed him to perform miracles for the Lord. One day Stephen preached to a crowd filled with hateful people who kept challenging his ideas. In the end, these men created lies about Stephen and his preaching and he was taken before the Sanhedrin, where he spoke the message of the Gospel to Saul and all the other Pharisees. Stephen was then sentenced to death by stoning and Saul oversaw this judgment and even held the coats of the men, who would fulfill this verdict. Stephen would become the first of many martyrs of the Church. Saul then began persecuting all the believers in Jerusalem. Many left the city, but the Apostles stayed. As Jon Courson states about this time in Saul's life, "The word "havoc" comes from a root word used to describe the results of wounding a wild boar. When a boar is wounded, he goes on a rampage and loses all sense of sanity—which is exactly what happened to Paul. This refined, cultured, religious scholar who sat at the feet of Gamaliel—this student par excellence, this man whose command of the Greek language was greater than any other writer—lost all sense of sanity. At first he merely consented to the death of Stephen. But then, like a shark that smells blood, he began going from house to house, hauling out and imprisoning believers, committing them to their deaths."[4]

After persecuting the believers in Jerusalem, Saul got permission from the High Priest and Jewish rabbi's from Damascus to go and persecute the Christians there and bring them back as prisoners. As Saul began his trip to Damascus with his group of blood-thirsty, persecuting men, he heard a great and mighty voice and then saw an amazing and spectacular light. As Saul heard and spoke to Jesus, the Light of the World, he believed in the Lord. Then his newfound Messiah instructed him to go to Damascus. The light Saul saw was so bright it blinded his eyes.

In his room, staring into the darkness, Saul was given time to search into his soul and repent. In Damascus, Ananias came to Saul to place his hands on him and Saul received the Holy Spirit. Suddenly scales fell off his eyes giving him the ability to see again. After receiving the Holy Spirit, Saul was baptized. After a time of discipleship, and only days later, he began preaching to the Jews. He kept preaching in Damascus, until he was forced to leave, because he was going to be killed.

Think of this time… Paul had just been killing Christians- now he was one of them. The people of Judea and the Christians were shocked not knowing whether to believe Paul's conversion. The Jews were stunned, while the Christians believed Paul was faking in order to know the whereabouts of the believers in Christ.

After fleeing for his life, Paul came to Jerusalem, where after a period of time, he was accepted and was discipled by the 12 Apostles and his future companion Barnabas. In Jerusalem, Paul debated with the scholars of the Jewish faith trying to tell them of the Messiah, but they were a stubborn people just like their ancestors before them and like their fore-fathers who complained in the wilderness for 40 years.

Paul was then taken away from Jerusalem to save his life and sent to Tarsus, his home, where he worked as a tent maker. Over time he felt compelled to share the Gospel. He had already fulfilled Acts 1:8 by preaching to Judea and Samaria first. Then he went to preach to Antioch (Syria) with Barnabas.

After preaching there, Paul was lead to go on four other missionary trips. To remember these trips use the following mnemonic " PACER."[5] P for Paul, A for Antioch (Turkey-1st Missionary trip; he travelled over 1400 miles), C for Corinth (Greece- 2nd Missionary trip; he travelled over 2800 miles), E for Ephesus (Turkey- 3rd Missionary trip; he travelled over 2700 miles), and R for Rome (Italy- 4th Missionary trip; he travelled over 2250 miles).

These missionary trips spanned a period of 30 years.

I Corinthians 15:32 talks about how Paul was almost killed on his third missionary journey in Ephesus, "If I fought wild beasts in Ephesus for merely human reasons, what have I gained? If the dead are not raised."[6] God may have saved Paul from the wild animals in an actual arena at Ephesus. Perhaps the event is factual, since the Bible declares how Paul was shielded from the lions. Another fact points to its reality, since many Christians were being eaten by lions at that time. However, the interrogative structure of Paul's statement brings into question the actuality of this event.

After returning from Turkey, Paul went to Jerusalem. Before he reached the city, Agabus, a prophet, prophesied that Paul would be turned over to the Gentiles by the Jews. Some of the Jewish Believers of the city wanted Paul to show the other Jewish Believers that he still followed the Law, so he went with them to the Temple to take part in a traditional ceremony. In the Temple, Paul was the witness of other men fulfilling their Nazarite vows. Paul fulfilled these same vows earlier in his life during his 2nd missionary trip. Acts 18:18-19 gives an account of this commitment, "So Paul still remained a good while. Then he took leave of the brethren and sailed for Syria, and Priscilla and Aquila were with him. He had his hair cut off at Cenchrea, for he had taken a vow."[7] Paul shaved his head and dedicated his hair to the Lord, which is believed to be a fulfillment of his Nazarite vows as the Law declares in Numbers 6.

Paul was still in the Temple, when some Asia minor Jews recognized him from his missionary trips. They condemned Paul by saying that he was against the Jews and the Law of Moses, because they believed he brought a Gentile into the Temple. This accusation was false. The crowd around the Temple burned with anger and they wanted to get their hands on Paul to kill him.

Paul was stationed with Roman soldiers to keep him safe from the rioters in Jerusalem. The Roman soldiers resolved to understand why there was rioting in the streets. They decided to flog Paul to secure this information. However, Paul was a Roman citizen and a citizen of Rome was always given a trial before punishment. Paul was tried before the Sanhedrin. Jews were outraged and intent on killing this "imposter," but God's hand was on him. God allowed his sister's son to hear about their plan and related it to Paul. The Romans didn't want any more trouble, so Paul was sent to Caesarea and was tried there.

He left for Caesarea, while it was still cloaked in darkness, because forty Jews were waiting to kill him. In Caesarea, Paul was put in prison for his own safety and was then presented before Governor Felix for his trial. The trial was not totally successful for nothing came out of the hearing. Paul was neither punished nor freed. Felix kept talking to Paul to try and get a bribe from him, but nothing happened. Paul stayed in prison two years, until Felix was replaced by Festus. This kept the Jews from rioting. Only a few days after Festus became governor, Jews from the Sanhedrin came to present their case to Festus. These Jews wanted Paul to be sent down to Jerusalem because they had another ambush set up. Festus declared that Paul was in Caesarea and that was where he would be tried. During the long heated trial, Paul was finally given a chance to speak and he requested to be sent to Caesarea, because he was a Roman citizen. Festus agreed. Shortly after the trial, King Agrippa II, ruler of a small territory in Judea, came to Caesarea to meet with Festus. He heard all about Paul's trial and wanted to hear this man for himself and his stories of Jesus. Paul was taken from the damp dungeon and brought before Festus and Agrippa. Paul shared his testimony of how he became a Christian. This is a good example for us. When we share the Gospel with people, it's good to share your own testimony. It leaves an indelible impression on others about the power of God in your life. After Paul completed his testimony, Agrippa stated that he was almost persuaded to become a Christian so Paul kept preaching to him. But Agrippa was so wrapped up in his sin and chose not to accept the Gospel. Agrippa told Festus, if Paul did not request to be sent to Rome, he would have been released. I believe it was God's will to have Paul sent to Caesar. Paul exclaimed how much he wanted to go to his fellow believers, who lived in Rome. God allowed Paul to be sent to Rome as a prisoner to allow His and Paul's will to be satisfied. Paul would have missed the opportunity to spread the Gospel to multitudes of people in Malta, Greece, Italy, Spain, and other regions he would preach to after being released from Nero's grip. Paul received his desire as well….to go to Spain(Romans 15:24)! God was glorified through Paul's evangelism and martyrdom. God's will was the BEST way!

A Roman ship took Paul on the long, arduous journey to Rome. Paul spent his time evangelizing to the prisoners and soldiers. During his journey, Paul prophesied that they would be shipwrecked, but no one would be hurt. The Lord allowed the ship to sink off the coast of Malta and not a single soul was wounded. God had a purpose through this event and it was revealed in the book of Acts. Paul was given the opportunity to preach for the cause of Christ. On the island, Paul experienced many miracles. While Paul was getting firewood, he was bitten by a venomous snake, but by God's providential hand, Paul didn't die. A sick man, whose name was Publius, and the rest of Malta's sick people were cured by God through Paul. This would be the only time in scripture where Paul would be seen healing people. After winter, all the shipwrecked souls headed to Rome. In Rome, Paul was welcomed by his brother and sisters in Christ. Paul was given a body guard who was there to protect him and keep him from escaping while under house arrest.

Paul met with the Jewish leaders in Rome and told them about the Messiah. Many believed. After this incident, the Bible only gives hints of the rest of Paul's life and the details of his other journeys. In Acts 28 we learn that he was imprisoned in Rome for two years. During this time, many of Paul's companions came to see him. He probably had many opportunities to preach to the Roman soldiers who guarded him. This is very important because the Roman soldiers were sent all across the known world. Many missionaries, because of the harsh conditions and constant wars, would not have the chance to go to these exotic countries such as France and England. However, many of these Roman soldiers were converted by Paul and other Apostles. In turn, when they were sent to fight for the Roman army, these soldiers were then given the chance to spread the Gospel to all the known world. The literal Roman Road, which the soldiers used, really did spread the Gospel to all places of the known world.

We learn another interesting fact in Acts 28. Paul was very well known in Rome by the Christian community. His first action in Rome was to preach the Gospel to his people, the Jews. From this point on in the life of Paul, there are only tidbits of information on Paul's life in the Bible, oral history, and the writings of the church fathers. Paul spent two years in Rome with his friends under house arrest. In Rome, he penned the epistles of Ephesians, Philippians, Colossians, and Philemon. These letters he sent to the Churches he evangelized to as well as his friend, Philemon. God's providence allowed Paul to be released and freed for a few years, which I believe follows the Biblical pattern of Paul's life. 2 Timothy 4:17 proves this. It declares "And I was delivered from the lion's mouth"[8] and the lion's mouth is Rome.

Once released, based upon biblical evidence, Paul went to preach God's word to Crete (Titus 1:5), Miletus (1Timothy 1:3), Colossae (Philemon 22), Troas (2nd Timothy 4:13), Philippi in Macedonia (Philippians 2:24 and 1st Timothy1:3), and Corinth (2nd Timothy 4:20). Once Paul's work was finished in these places, God's will was once again fulfilled.

God's will was written by Paul in Romans 15:22-24, 28 where he states to the Romans in the Roman church, "This is why I have often been hindered from coming to you. But now that there is no more place for me to work in these regions, and since I have been longing for many years to see you, I plan to do so when I go to Spain. I hope to visit you while passing through and to have you assist me on my journey there, after I have enjoyed your company for a while."[9]… (v28) " So after I have completed this task and have made sure they have received this fruit, I will to Spain and visit you on they way."[10] In this verse, Paul shows his yearning to go and preach the gospel to Spain and many theologians believe he finally accomplished God's will. One such pastor, Jon Courson states, "Paul planned to go to Spain (verse 24). Did he ever make it? We don't know. Church tradition indicates he did, indeed, go to Spain..… But this can't be emphatically verified. I personally believe he did go to Spain. Why? Because right before his death, he wrote, 'I have finished my course' (2Timothy 4:7)."[11] Many church fathers wrote of Paul's visit to Spain. One proof of Paul visiting Spain is verified by the church father, Clement, who writes of the journey of Paul. Clement, the first Bishop (leader) of the

Roman Church, states in his 1st Epistle to the Corinthians 5:5, "Paul, too, showed.......he obtained the noble renown due to his faith; and having preached righteousness to the whole world, and having come to the extremity of the West....."[12] The extremity of the west in ancient times was Spain and this quote was written only 20-30 years after Paul's journey to Spain.

After preaching and making disciples in Spain, one of two events happened. Paul may have gone back to all the places he preached, after his two year imprisonment or he may have been taken back to Rome as a prisoner. Either way, Paul sooner or later was imprisoned again in Rome. There is a separate theory about what Paul did in this time period, which says he went to France or England as a missionary. I did not include such ideas, because there is no biblical basis for it. Such written accounts were recorded 300-400 years after the life of Paul. The information could have been altered, since it was written long after these events. Many in these remote areas became believers in

Jesus through the work of Roman soldiers, not Paul. The Gospel, The Roman Road, was spoken to the world by Roman soldiers on Roman roads.

Once his mission in Spain was completed, which lasted about a year, he was forcefully imprisoned by Emperor Nero a second time. This second imprisonment in Rome was harsher than the first. Many historians believe Paul went to Rome on his free will to preach. However, when a fire destroyed Rome in 64 A.D. Nero blamed it on the Christians. This event created great persecution and was most likely the reason why Paul was imprisoned.

Paul's prison was probably an underground pit, where Roman soldiers would guard him. In this prison there was an opening the size of your waist that allowed rain to wash animal waste into the hole. To say the least, this created a strong odor! Paul's prison didn't have any bathrooms creating an even more unbearable smell and there may also have been a lack of food and bedding.

2nd Timothy was written while Paul was in prison and states that Alexander from Ephesus, a coppersmith, exhibited evil acts against this Apostle. Alexander may have been one of the causes that put Paul in prison, since this was written while he was in his underground pit.

In the dimly lighted prison, Paul was given many chances to preach to his guards and to write many epistles including 1st and 2nd Timothy, but in this prison Paul was very lonely. In 2nd Timothy 4:11 he states, "Only Luke is with me."[13] To me, this sounds as if he misses his other disciples.

Paul was brought before Nero more than once. In 2 Timothy 4:16 Paul writes, "At my first defense, no one came to my support, but everyone deserted me."[14] Paul is mentioning his first of many trials in which he proclaimed and defended the Gospel all alone in front of Caesar. Paul was not afraid to talk before Caesar and therefore believed the fear of man is a snare, but we should only fear (honor) God. Nero decided in court, by the hand of the devil, that Paul was to be put to death as a Roman citizen. Paul was most likely in prison for a shorter amount of time than his first imprisonment because Nero was a madman killing Christians every day. One account even states he put believers of Jesus on stakes and lit them on fire like candles to guide his path when he went chariot riding at night fully naked. When Paul knew he was about to martyred, he begged Timothy and Mark, whom he loved very much, to come quickly so he could see them one more time before he died. Paul says in 2 Timothy 4:9, "Do your best to come to me quickly."[15] History never tells us, if Paul got his final wish. Second Timothy is the last time Paul is heard from in the Bible and soon after he may have been martyred.

The story of his martyrdom is interesting because some historians believe Paul and Nero died the same year. Both of these men are exact opposites of each other. Paul loved God and cared for others, while Nero was a pagan who cared only for himself and was controlled by demonic beings. Paul was martyred. Nero took his life by suicide. Paul and

Nero are exact opposites. The greatest difference
is evidenced in that Paul is in Heaven, while Nero is
in Hell.

Paul, on that fateful day, was taken from the dimly
lit prison and out into Rome's bustling city of
traders, high and low class citizens and foreigners.
Paul was then most likely followed by his friends,
converts, and other believers in Christ, as he was
taken to an executioner. Before Paul died he stated
in 2nd Timothy 4:18, "The Lord will rescue me from
every evil attack and will bring me safely to his
heavenly kingdom. To him be glory for ever and
ever. Amen."[16] I believe God did rescue Paul from
evil by taking him out of the evil surrounding him.
Sometimes, God answers our prayers, but in ways
we don't get or understand. As Paul was taken to
the executioner his thoughts were racing, but his
eyes were on his imminent departure from this
Earth and his coming arrival into Heaven. Paul was
to be beheaded, since Roman citizens were given
the privilege of a less painful death. Paul's head
was placed upon a stump of wood. His throat,

which spoke of the Gospel for decades, was penetrated by the honed, iron sword, which then decapitated the old, white-headed man, who spent his life in humility, service, and love for the Lord.

Paul had finished his race with flying colors for the Lord. He walked with God and spread the Gospel throughout the known world to the Jews and Gentiles. The apostle had fulfilled the Great Commission that Jesus gave to every man and woman, who has a true relationship with the Messiah. His life is an amazing example of how we should live out our life in Christ. As the executioner completed God's plan of Paul's martyrdom, he was taken to his final, permanent home, Heaven. John 14:3 explains Paul's journey to his final home. "I come back and take you to be with me that you also may be where I am."[17] Luke 23:43 says, " I tell you the truth, today you will be with me in Paradise."[18] As the blade struck his earthly body, he was brought to Heaven and saw God's Glory and Holiness. Paul now has peace in Heaven, sitting in God's presence, enjoying his eternal home and praising God! In Paul's own word's 1 Corinthians 2:9 tells us, " No eye has seen, nor ear heard, nor the heart of man imagined, what God has prepared for those who love him."[19]

Jesus has honored Paul, because he blesses those who bless Him. Paul worked for the glory of the Lord and he got his greatest reward, martyrdom. As Philippians 1:21 says, "For to me, to live is Christ and to die is gain."[20] Paul's life as he has stated in scripture was a race. Who was he racing against? Himself. Why? Paul wanted the best: to give the most glory to God, the best for himself, and the most blessings to others. Paul finished the race by giving his life away, but it was not in vain. It was for the glory of God, the good of others, and it brought Paul to Heaven.

Paul repeatedly states he must win the "prize." What was the prize? To fulfill his life as a child of God and to honor God with his Heavenly reward. Happiness comes though God's will and brings everlasting joy. Paul states in Philippians 3:14, "I press on toward the goal to win the prize for which God has called me heavenward in Christ Jesus."[21] Paul pressed on to his goal. He would fall, but he always got back up. Paul trudged forward in God and in the end received the prize of eternity with Jesus Christ, his and our Lord and Savior. Paul, just before he died, was content to declare in 2nd Timothy 4:7, "I have fought the good fight, I have finished the race, I have kept the faith."[22]

Conclusion

"Then I heard the voice of the Lord
saying, "Whom shall I send? And who
will go for us?" And I said,
"Here am I. Send me!""
Isaiah, Israelite prophet from the
8th century B.C.

Ten out of Ten people die. This statistical fact will never change until the Church is raptured, but until then, we are racing against time. Hopefully, from this book you will have seen how believers in Christ from the first century used their time on Earth for importance, even dying for the cause of Christ. Peter, Paul, and all the rest had a deep understanding that time was against them and they had a mission given to them by Jesus (Matthew 28: 16-20), which had to and was fulfilled by each one of these amazing men. This mission has not been finished. It is to share the Gospel to every one from Judea, Samaria, and to all the world. The Great Commission is passed on to each one of us, when we become saved through His blood. Once that declaration is made, the mission for Christ begins.

In our Present-day world, over 160,000 believers in Jesus have taken this mission to heart and have died as a martyr for our Lord each year. In the non-Christian world there are only about 2-3 million missionaries out of the two billion Christians in the entire world. This is only .001% of the Christian population. I believe Jesus wants more believers to be bold and not fall in the face of fear when sharing the Gospel of Salvation. The Apostles of Christ loved the Lord with their whole hearts and would go anywhere or do anything for Jesus. Believers in Christ, during the 21st century should whole-heartedly choose to share the Gospel and remember to give God the glory since we can do nothing without the Creator. Take heed, time is a wasting and you need to choose to work as disciples of the Lord to bring the news that there is a way to eternal life… Jesus! As Benjamin Franklin wisely and cleverly states, " Lost time is never found again."[1] Time is of the essence, because today may be our last and I would hope that we shall all hear Jesus say, "Well done, good and faithful servant!"[2]

These Apostles teach us to pray for all of the believers in Christ who are imprisoned or being persecuted. The power of a Christian prayer is seen in the Bible, when Peter was in prison and the Lord supernaturally liberated him (Acts 12). God wants us to pray for the persecuted. Hebrews 13:3 states, " Continue to remember those in prison as if you were together with them in prison, and those who are mistreated as if you yourselves were suffering."[3] God listens to all of our prayers and, if they are in the will of the Almighty, He will answer them according to His plans.

The Apostles of the 1st century prove the death and resurrection of Jesus. Many believe that the twelve Disciples stole the body of the Savior. Who would die for a man who lied and was the same as any of them? These Apostles died for the Gospel, which is truth. Not a single person would die for what they knew to be a lie. Chuck Colson states, " I know the resurrection is a fact, and Watergate proved it to me. How? Because 12 men testified they had seen Jesus raised from the dead, then they proclaimed that truth for 40 years, never once denying it. Every one was beaten, tortured, stoned and put in prison. They would not have endured that if it weren't true. Watergate embroiled 12 of the most powerful men in the world-and they couldn't keep a lie for three weeks. You're telling me 12 apostles could keep a lie for 40 years? Absolutely impossible."[4]

Once Jesus came to Earth, it never was, is, or will be the same! Think of the absolute craziness of fishermen, tax collectors, scholars, zealots, and all the rest, who literally turned the world up side down for God's glory. Amazingly, these Galileans went throughout the world preaching the Gospel to everyone and changed life forever. This is extraordinary and shows how God can use anyone, including you and me, to get His plan completed. As I have studied the lives of Christ's Apostles, I have come to the understanding that all will work together for good and fit into God's plans.

Jesus loves mankind, who take up only the corner of His Universe. He made all things including you. Jesus, the One who created the atom, one of the smallest particles of matter in the universe, and the One who created the star UY Scuti, which could contain 5 billion suns. Yet Jesus loves us the most! His love is so great He allowed people to mock

Him, beat Him, and kill Him. Yet He did it for you. This should make you jump for joy that Jesus loves you more than anything else in all Creation!

The disciples faced horrendous deaths because they knew all that the pain had to offer was not more than the joy they were to receive in Heaven. This joy came from Jesus. I would like to show you how much God loves you by examining some of the sufferings the eternal Creator experienced.

Jesus was crucified around 30 A.D. Most historians claim it to be the most horrific death in all history. In its original language crucifixion means "excruciating." The act of crucifying a person was used in 400 B.C. by the Persians. Many historians now believe that the Assyrians started this practice hundreds of years before. In the year 722 B.C., the Assyrians took the Israelites captive. To annihilate this nation, they placed a sharp stake up through their body and left them on the pole until they died. This may have been an early form of crucifixion. Over time many empires used this practice. The

Greeks and the Romans perfected the act of crucification by making it even more intolerable, which was and is still used in modern times by the Muslims, Japanese, and some current-day countries such as Sudan and Burma.

When Jesus was taken by the Romans, He was pummeled in His face so badly that He was unrecognizable. He was whipped thirty-nine times with a Cat-of-nine tails. This torture tool had shards of glass attached to each of the nine pieces of leather and ripped the flesh off His back. When He was finally led to Golgotha, He was forced to carry His cross, which was 75-125 pounds and was tied around his neck and shoulders.

When Jesus was at Golgotha his wrists were nailed to the cross, which would have destroyed the nerves running through his arm. His body was not vertical on the cross, but in a more excruciating position. His legs and calves where at a 90 degree angle. On the cross, Jesus would have to push on his lower body to breathe bringing more pain to our

Lord, since he had 5-7 inch nails in his feet. As Jesus breathed, his lower body would not have the strength to take all of his weight in that position on the cross. Over time his legs would collapse from cramps and exhaustion. This would then force Jesus' upper body to slouch, pulling his shoulders out of their sockets and making his arms 9 inches longer, which put more pressure on his wrists. During a period of six hours, Jesus experienced physical torture, the wrath for our sins (past, present, and future), and rejection by His Father, God. The Lord's heart began to beat faster than normal, because his blood was deoxygenated. This situation produced fatigue, since his cells could not produce energy from a lack of oxygen. Jesus would then struggle even more to breathe as He let out carbon dioxide. His breathing became heavier and faster. Then Jesus' blood pressure would have droppod, oinoo Ho hadn't had fluids for 15 hours and He would have been dizzy. Over a span of time, Jesus' heart would have been surrounded by plasma and blood forcing his heart to slow down. All of this pressure from the fluids covering his heart would have been so much that his heart actually ruptured. The rupturing of his heart would have been the cause of his death. This is the reason why water and blood poured out of Jesus' body when the Roman soldier rammed the spear into his side. I believe Jesus' heart rupturing is symbolic, because biblically the *heart* represents a person's center for both physical and emotional-intellectual-moral activities.[5] When the Lord's heart ruptured, it also burst spiritually from all the pain he felt by experiencing all of our sins.

Understanding all that Jesus did for the disciples, for you, and for me creates a deep love and passion for Him; the One who gave us the gift of eternal life with our Creator. As Isaiah 53:5-6 declares, "But He was pierced for our transgressions, He was crushed for our iniquities; the punishment that brought us peace was on him, and by his wounds we are healed. We all, like sheep, have gone astray, each of us has turned to our own way; and the Lord has laid on Him the iniquity of us all."[6]

I have explained only a few of the many horrendous tortures Jesus had to experience for the salvation of mankind. From the apostles' lives, I hope you see the love of Jesus for all the world. John 3:16 says, " For God so loved the world that He gave His only begotten Son, that whoever believes in Him shall not perish but have everlasting life."[7] Jesus loves us so much he died for our sins, making us perfect to live with Him forever.

Even though He died, He rose from the dead and now is alive, living with each one of us in our walk with Him. As 2nd Peter 3:18 proclaims, " To Him be glory both now and forever! Amen." [8] "' Yes, I am coming soon.' Amen. Come, Lord Jesus. (May) The grace of the Lord be with all God's people. Amen. (Revelation 22:20b-21)"[9]

Notes

Introduction
1. The Holy Bible, New International Version. Grand Rapids, 1984. Print., p. 878
2. Ibid., p. 826
3. Ibid., p. 878
4. " Martyr." dictionary.com. Dictionary, 2013. Web. 14 January, 2013
5. The Holy Bible, New International Version. Grand Rapids, 1984. Print., p. 1020

Chapter 1
James, the Son of Zebedee
1. The Holy Bible, New International Version. Grand Rapids, 1984. Print., p. 835
2. Ibid., p. 919
3. Lockyer, Herbert. All the Apostles of the Bible. Grand Rapids; Zondervan Publishing House, 1972. Print., p. 251
4. The Holy Bible, New International Version. Grand Rapids, 1984. Print., p. 844
5. Ibid., p. 977

Chapter 2
Peter or Simon, the son of Jonas,
1. Courson, Jon. Jon Courson's Application Commentary. Nashville; Thomas Nelson, Inc, 2006. Print., p. 711

2. Lockyer, Herbert. All the Apostles of the Bible. Grand Rapids; Zondervan Publishing House, 1972. Print., p. 257
3. Ibid., p. 257
4. The Holy Bible, New International Version. Grand Rapids, 1984. Print., p. 907

Chapter 3
John, the Son of Zebedee

1. Lockyer, Herbert. All the Apostles of the Bible. Grand Rapids; Zondervan Publishing House, 1972. Print., p. 252
2. Courson, Jon. Jon Courson's Application Commentary. Nashville; Thomas Nelson, Inc, 2006. Print., p. 607
3. Lockyer, Herbert. All the Apostles of the Bible. Grand Rapids; Zondervan Publishing House, 1972. Print., p. 253
4. The Holy Bible, New International Version. Grand Rapids, 1984. Print., p.827

Chapter 4
Simon the Zealot

1. Courson, Jon. Jon Courson's Application Commentary. Nashville; Thomas Nelson, Inc, 2006. Print., p. 73
2. Rose Publishing. The Twelve Disciples. Torrance: Rose Publishing, 2004. Print.,
3. Lockyer, Herbert. All the Apostles of the Bible. Grand Rapids; Zondervan Publishing House, 1972. Print., p. 259

Chapter 5
Thomas
1. Courson, Jon. Jon Courson's Application Commentary. Nashville; Thomas Nelson, Inc, 2006. Print., p. 533
2. The Holy Bible, New International Version. Grand Rapids, 1984. Print., p. 906
3. Ibid., p. 906
4. Lockyer, Herbert. All the Apostles of the Bible. Grand Rapids; Zondervan Publishing House, 1972. Print., p. 260

Chapter 6
Matthias
1. Braght, Thieleman. Martyr's Mirror. Scottdale; Herald Press,1660. Website, p. 93
2. The Holy Bible, New International Version. Grand Rapids, 1984. Print., p. 865
3. Courson, Jon. Jon Courson's Application Commentary. Nashville; Thomas Nelson, Inc, 2006. Print., p. 613

Chapter 7
Matthew(Levi), Son of Alphaeus
1. Rose Publishing. The Twelve Disciples. Torrance: Rose Publishing, 2004. Print
2. Down, David. Unveiling the Kings of Israel. Green Forest; Master Books, 2012. Print., p. 153

3. "Bible Characters: Matthew A Disciple." essortment.com. Website, 2013. Web. 26 May, 2013
4. The Holy Bible, New International Version. Grand Rapids, 1984. Print., p. 938
5. "Bible Characters: Matthew A Disciple." essortment.com. Website, 2013. Web. 26 May, 2013

Chapter 8
Bartholomew(Nathanael)

1. Braght, Thieleman. Martyr's Mirror. Scottdale; Herald Press, 1660. Website, p. 89
2. Courson, Jon. Jon Courson's Application Commentary. Nashville; Thomas Nelson, Inc, 2006. Print., p. 443
3. The Holy Bible, New International Version. Grand Rapids, 1984. Print., p. 885
4. The Holy Bible, New International Version. Grand Rapids, 1984. Print., p.885
5. Rose Publishing. The Twelve Disciples. Torrance: Rose Publishing, 2004. Print
6. Braght, Thieleman. Martyr's Mirror. Scottdale; Herald Press, 1660. Website, p. 89
7. Ibid., p. 90

Chapter 9
Philip

1. Rose Publishing. The Twelve Disciples. Torrance: Rose Publishing, 2004. Print

2. Braght, Thieleman. Martyr's Mirror. Scottdale; Herald Press, 1660. Website, p. 75
3. Lockyer, Herbert. All the Apostles of the Bible. Grand Rapids; Zondervan Publishing House, 1972. Print., p. 259
4. The Holy Bible, New International Version. Grand Rapids, 1984. Print., p.907
5. Ibid., p. 832
6. Ibid., p. 811

Chapter 10
Andrew

1. The Holy Bible, New International Version. Grand Rapids, 1984. Print., p.885
2. Ibid., p. 885
3. Ibid., p. 907
4. Braght, Thieleman. Martyr's Mirror. Scottdale; Herald Press, 1660. Website, p. 89
5. Ibid., p. 89
6. Ibid., p. 89
7. Ibid., p. 89
8. Ibid., p.89
9. Ibid., p 89

Chapter 11
James, the Son of Alpaeus

1. The Holy Bible, New International Version. Grand Rapids, 1984. Print., p.834
2. Ibid., p. 811

3. Ibid., p.829
4. Rose Publishing. The Twelve Disciples. Torrance: Rose Publishing, 2004. Print

Chapter 12
Thaddeus, also known as Judas
1. The Holy Bible, New International Version. Grand Rapids, 1984. Print., p.900
2. Rose Publishing. The Twelve Disciples. Torrance: Rose Publishing, 2004. Print

Chapter 13
James, the Brother of Jesus
1. The Holy Bible, New International Version. Grand Rapids, 1984. Print., p.838
2. Ibid., p. 7
3. Courson, Jon. Jon Courson's Application Commentary. Nashville; Thomas Nelson, Inc, 2006. Print., p.498
4. "Prayer Quotes." http://hopefaithprayer.com/prayernew/prayer-quotes/. Website, 2015, Web 6 January, 2015
5. Lockyer, Herbert. All the Apostles of the Bible. Grand Rapids; Zondervan Publishing House, 1972. Print., p.251

Chapter 14
Paul, the Apostle
1. The Holy Bible, New International Version. Grand Rapids, 1984. Print., p.

2. Ibid., p.
3. Courson, Jon. Jon Courson's Application Commentary. Nashville; Thomas Nelson, Inc, 2006. Print., p.
4. Ibid., p.
5. Rose Publishing. The Twelve Disciples. Torrance: Rose Publishing, 2004. Print.
6. The Holy Bible, New International Version. Grand Rapids, 1984. Print., p.
7. Ibid., p.
8. Ibid., p.
9. Ibid., p.
10. Ibid., p.
11. Courson, Jon. Jon Courson's Application Commentary. Nashville; Thomas Nelson, Inc, 2006. Print., p.
12. "St.Clement of Rome: First Epistles to the Corinthians." http://www.voskrese.info/spl/CleRom1Cor5.html
13. The Holy Bible, New International Version. Grand Rapids, 1984. Print., p.
14. Ibid., p.
15. Ibid., p.
16. Ibid., p.
17. Ibid., p.
18. Ibid., p.
19. Ibid., p.
20. Ibid., p.
21. Ibid., p.
22. Ibid., p.

Conclusion

1. "Benjamin Franklin Quotes." http://www.brainyquote.com/quotes/quotes/b/benjaminfr104457.html. Website, 2015, Web. 7 January, 2015

2. The Holy Bible, New International Version. Grand Rapids, 1984. Print., p.827

3. Ibid., p. 1003

4. " Chuck Colson on the Resurrection." http://www.faithvillage.com/blogpost/856ea5b55d70480084008717c026987d/chuck_colson_on_the_resurrection. Website, 2015, Web. 7 January, 2015

5. "Heart." http://www.biblestudytools.com/dictionary/heart/. Website, 2015, Web. 7 January, 2015

6. The Holy Bible, New International Version. Grand Rapids, 1984. Print., p.617

7. Ibid., p. 886

8. Ibid., p. 1013

9. Ibid., p. 1034

Bibliography

1. "Benjamin Franklin Quotes." http://
www.brainyquote.com/quotes/quotes/b/
benjaminfr104457.html. Website, 2015, Web. 7
January, 2015

2."Bible Characters: Matthew A Disciple."
essortment.com. Website, 2013. Web. 26 May,
2013

3.Braght, Thieleman. Martyr's Mirror. Scottdale;
Herald Press, 1660. Website

4. " Chuck Colson on the Resurrection." http://
www.faithvillage.com/blogpost/
856ea5b55d70480084008717c026987d/
chuck_colson_on_the_resurrection. Website,
2015,

5. Courson, Jon. Jon Courson's Application
Commentary. Nashville; Thomas Nelson, Inc,
2006. Print.

6. Down, David. Unveiling the Kings of Israel.
Green Forest; Master Books, 2012. Print.

7. "Heart." http://www.biblestudytools.com/
dictionary/heart/. Website, 2015, Web. 7 January,
2015

8. Lockyer, Herbert. All the Apostles of the Bible.
Grand Rapids; Zondervan Publishing House,
1972. Print.

9. " Martyr." dictionary.com. Dictionary, 2013.
Web. 14 January, 2013

10. "Prayer Quotes." http://hopefaithprayer.com/prayernew/prayer-quotes/. Website, 2015, Web 6 January, 2015

11. The Holy Bible, New International Version. Grand Rapids, 1984. Print.

12. Rose Publishing. The Twelve Disciples. Torrance: Rose Publishing, 2004. Print.

13. "St.Clement of Rome: First Epistles to the Corinthians." http://www.voskrese.info/spl/CleRom1Cor5.html. Website, 2015,

25916300R00075

Made in the USA
Middletown, DE
15 November 2015